P9-DWJ-368

Culinary Journey to the Mediterranean

Come take a culinary voyage through the kitchens of the vast area that surrounds the Mediterranean sea.
Discover great-tasting foods filled with the region's vibrant aromas and flavors. While the well-known dishes of Italy and the South of France may be the most familiar, there's so much more to discover.

Before your journey, learn about the ingredients commonly used in Mediterranean cooking. Then, venture through the mouthwatering collection of 56 easy-to-prepare recipes.

Included are recipes featuring DI GIORNO and ATHENOS cheeses, ATHENOS Mediterranean Spreads, COLAVITA Olive Oil and Vinegar, and California Walnuts and Olives—all easily found ingredients that bring great taste to Mediterranean cooking.

From appealing appetizers to delicious desserts, the recipes offer an introduction to the cuisine of this fascinating part of the world. Come see how the foods of the Mediterranean can bring so much pleasure to your table. Bon Voyage!

©Copyright 1997 Churny Company, Inc. ©Copyright 1997 Meredith Corporation. All rights reserved. Printed in Hong Kong.
Produced by Meredith Custom Publishing, 1912 Grand Ave., Des Moines, Iowa 50309-3379.
ATHENOS, DI GIORNO, PHILADELPHIA BRAND and KRAFT Mayo are registered trademarks of Kraft Foods, Inc. COLAVITA is a registered trademark of Colavita Olive Oil.

Pictured on front cover: Mostaccioli with Spinach & Feta (recipe, page 37)

Culinary Journey to the Mediterranean

Mediterranean

greece

TuRKey

ean Sea

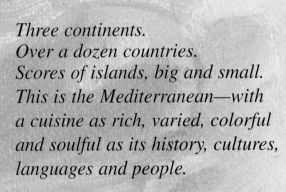

Three continents.
Over a dozen countries.
Scores of islands, big and small.
This is the Mediterranean—with
a cuisine as rich, varied, colorful
and soulful as its history, cultures,
languages and people.

The ingredients that make up this cuisine reflect the generous diversity of this vast geographical sweep. Some of these foods, such as seafood, find their way into dishes throughout the region. Other ingredients, such as North Africa's couscous, are a specialty of a particular region.

This chapter surveys some of the most common ingredients found in Mediterranean kitchens—foods that lend invigorating aromas and robust flavors to this multinational fare. And contrary to what you might think, the items are not difficult to find. You may be surprised to discover that you already have many of them in your own kitchen pantry.

Vegetables

Because vegetables grow well in the warm, sunny climate of the Mediterranean, they make up a large part of the daily diet. Eggplants and tomatoes are two of the region's culinary hallmarks. Plum tomatoes are excellent choices for sauces. Tomatoes also star in Panzanella (pahn-zah-NEHL-lah), an Italian tomato and bread salad; a version of this recipe, called Rustic Bread Salad, is on page 54. A celebrated dish featuring eggplant is France's ratatouille (rah-tah-TOO-ee), a mélange of Mediterranean vegetables. Multipurpose bell peppers show up in soups, stews, sauces and salads. Crunchy fennel is eaten raw in salads or cooked with other vegetables or fish. Wild porcini mushrooms are often sautéed in olive oil along with garlic and herbs. Other vegetables of the area include artichokes, zucchini and onions.

Fruits

Fruits, fresh and dried, make an appearance at nearly every Mediterranean meal in both savory and sweet dishes. Figs are grown all over the Mediterranean region. Cooks' creations include rolling prosciutto (proh-SHOO-toh) around fig halves as an antipasto, poaching figs in compotes or baking them in tarts and cakes for dessert. Dates, grown in the desert of North Africa, are stuffed in fish, put into couscous, and added to salads and stews. Peaches, plums, apricots, oranges, tangerines, grapes, lemons and limes have all made their mark in Mediterranean cuisine, and not only in desserts. Many soups, stews, and fish and poultry dishes are highlighted with these fruits, as is sangria (san-GREE-uh), the fruity Spanish wine beverage.

CHeeses

Cheeses add plenty of flavor to a variety of recipes, from appetizers to desserts. Feta (FEH-tuh), a white, semisoft, crumbly cheese is a favorite of Mediterranean cooks. **ATHENOS Feta Cheeses** are often crumbled in salads as well as used in cooking. Whether enjoying traditional feta cheese, or Basil & Tomato, Garlic & Herb, or Peppercorn varieties, the distinctive flavor of feta adds a special note to the overall dish. In another form, **ATHENOS Mediterranean Spreads** capture the taste of feta cheese in a spreadable consistency.

Then there is the unsurpassable Parmesan cheese, called parmigiano (pahr-mih-JAH-noh) in Italian. **DI GIORNO Parmesan Cheese,** with its rich, sharp flavor, is most often used grated or shredded over pasta, rice and soups. Romano, another Italian cheese, has a slightly sharper flavor. A cousin to Romano is Pecorino Romano; it's made with sheep's milk while Romano is made with cow's milk. Use shredded or grated **DI GIORNO Romano** and **Pecorino Romano** like Parmesan.

And don't forget the mildly flavored mozzarella cheese—a favorite with pizza and baked pasta dishes. Goat cheese is also available, and both mozzarella and goat cheese are often marinated in olive oil or coated with herbs or pepper.

These cheeses vary in their popularity throughout the regions. For example, Greece loves its feta, Italy favors Parmesan and Romano, while goat cheese is found more often in France.

grains and Legumes

These versatile ingredients are truly the staff of life in Mediterranean cooking, providing a hearty foundation that ensures each meal satisfies. Because meat is of secondary importance in the Mediterranean diet, grains and legumes are a significant source of protein.

Cooks all around the region have been using grains in a vast array of shapes and sizes for centuries. Consider bulgur, a cracked wheat product most often used in pilafs or side dishes such as the Middle Eastern salad, tabbouleh (tuh-BOO-luh). And, contrary to popular belief, Italy doesn't corner the

CALifoRNia

FRench Niçoise

DRied Black

Ripe

Spanish gReen

Sicilian

KaLaMata

market on pasta—residents of Spain and the eastern Mediterranean also enjoy this satisfying staple.

Rice finds its way onto Mediterranean tables as well. Special varieties include basmati, a nutty-tasting, long-grain rice, and Italy's short-grain arborio rice, called for in some risotto (rih-SAW-toh) recipes.

Sail across the sea to North Africa, and you'll find couscous (KOOS-koos), this area's signature grain product, made from ground semolina. It's commonly steamed and served with stews.

As for legumes, inhabitants of the Mediterranean basin enjoy them in healthful and imaginative ways. Lentils have been used in the area since biblical times. Today, you'll find them used as the base for soups and stews, as well as in salads. Garbanzo beans—also called chickpeas—are a hearty legume included in salads, soups and stews. They're also an important ingredient of the classic Middle Eastern favorite, hummus (HUH-muhs). **ATHENOS Mediterranean Spreads**—original and flavored hummus—also are available and are ready to use.

Other classic beans include fava beans (sometimes called broad beans) and white beans (including both navy beans and great northern beans). Both are enjoyed in a variety of soups and salads, and white beans are also featured in casseroles. In Italy, creamy white cannellini (kan-eh-LEE-nee) beans are a favorite in a number of classic dishes.

Olive Oil

Olive oil has a rich history that is centuries old. Referred to as olio di oliva (OH-lyoh dee o-LEE-vah) in Italian, it's one of the cornerstones of cooking in the Mediterranean, where it is used as an ingredient, flavor enhancer and cooking medium. Olive oils take on characteristic tastes, depending on where the olives were grown, the type and quality of the fruit, time of harvest, weather during the growing season and how they are produced. There are basically only two types of oil available to consumers. Extra virgin is the highest quality, fresh-squeezed "juice" of the olive. **COLAVITA Extra Virgin**

Olive Oil has a green-gold color and flavor suitable for a variety of culinary uses. The other type of oil is ordinary or "pure" olive oil, and its cousin "light" olive oil. (Light olive oil refers to taste and color, not the caloric and fat content.) **COLAVITA Pure Olive Oil** is enriched with COLAVITA virgin olive oil for taste and aroma.

Olives

Because of their various tastes, textures and aromas, olives offer endless possibilities for adding variety to Mediterranean dishes. **California Ripe Olives,** with their mild, almost nutlike flavor, are great for snacking, and are an excellent addition to recipes. They are available year-round in a range of sizes and can be bought pitted, sliced or chopped. Spanish green olives come stuffed with pimientos, almonds or other delicious additions. Their distinctive tangy and tart flavor also makes them a favorite snack food. Kalamata (or Calamata) olives from Greece have a distinctive black-purple color and pointed ends—they're the traditional addition to a Greek salad. Dried black olives from Greece or Italy, Sicilian olives from California or Italy, and French Niçoise (nee-SWAHZ) olives all have strong olive or salty flavors. These olives are usually sold unpitted.

Nuts and SEEDs

Throughout the Mediterranean, nuts are, and have been for centuries, a common snack. They're also used extensively in cooking and baking as well. Given their versatility and lush flavor, it's no wonder walnuts have been lending their rich character to the foods of the Mediterranean for centuries. Even though the walnuts most commonly found in the United States are referred to as "English" walnuts, we tend to call them **California Walnuts** to designate their current geographical place of origin. In Mediterranean cooking today, walnuts make fabulous sauces and salad additions. They also enrich pastries.

Almonds and almond paste are also popular in Mediterranean pastries, and ground almonds often thicken soups and stews. Pine nuts are used in dishes, both sweet and savory, such as pesto. Pistachio nuts also are used. Sesame seeds often are sprinkled on vegetables and sweet dishes for flavor and as a garnish, or ground into a paste called tahini (tuh-HEE-nee).

Fish and SHellfish

The Mediterranean's azure waters are the source of many culinary treasures. A visit to a Mediterranean fish market reveals a staggering variety of fish and shellfish that make their way into restaurants and homes in a repertoire of grilled, fried, baked and braised fish dishes. Other distinctive dishes include an array of fish and seafood soups and stews, such as Zuppa di Pesce (TSOO-puh dee PAY-shay).

MEAts and POUltry

While meat did not play a significant role on Mediterranean menus of yesterday, it shows up more and more on today's tables. Lamb, associated with kabobs, is popular throughout the eastern Mediterranean. A leg of lamb is often served on special occasions. Pork is most often cured and made into ham or sausages. Occasionally beef and veal are featured in some Mediterranean dishes. Grilled, braised and roasted poultry dishes are served with little embellishment.

Herbs and SPices

While the most expensive of all spices, saffron, is an essential ingredient in esteemed rice and seafood dishes throughout the Mediterranean, other herbs and spices are tell-tale specialties of a particular region. Middle Eastern and North African cuisines both use parsley, mint, dill and cilantro to make their foods come alive. Yet the two cuisines have some remarkable differences: sweet spices like cinnamon and allspice offer spice without heat to North African dishes, while Middle Eastern cuisines favor more earthy spices like cumin and coriander seeds.

Across the blue waters, countries along the northern shores accent their specialties with basil—pesto being one of the most common—and oregano, which adds zest to pizza and other regional specialties. Other favorite seasonings include rosemary, which grows wild in the Mediterranean area, and thyme.

BASIL

PARSLEY

Rosemary

CUminSeeds

When preparing recipes, if you have access to fresh herbs, use them instead of the dried—just triple the amount called for in your recipe. For example, if a recipe uses 1 teaspoon dried herb, add 3 teaspoons (1 tablespoon) snipped fresh herb.

Additional SEASonings

No list of Mediterranean seasonings would be complete without garlic. Italian cooks use it generously and it plays a vital role in other southern European and Middle Eastern cuisines.

Tiny green capers add a pickled, salty and pungent flavor to a variety of Mediterranean salads, fish entrées, sauces and relishes. Although not as common in America, harissa (hah-REE-suh) is a notable ingredient in North African dishes; use this fiery paste, made from pounded red chili peppers, with caution because it's very hot. Use only small amounts of

tahini as well. Tahini is a thick paste made of ground sesame seed that's used to flavor Middle Eastern dishes, most notably hummus. **ATHENOS Mediterranean Spreads** have many flavors of ready-to-eat hummus.

Vinegars, referred to as aceto (ah-CHAY-toh) in Italian, are an indispensable staple in Mediterranean fare. Red, white and sherry vinegars are used in dressings, in marinades and for pickling. One specialty vinegar, **COLAVITA Balsamic Vinegar,** is a thick, strong-flavored vinegar used in salads. It's dark brown and has full-bodied flavor.

And finally, Mediterranean cooks not only like to serve a good bottle of dry red or white wine to accompany a meal, but also use it to flavor their stews, marinades and sauces as well.

starters

People who live in countries bordering the Mediterranean Sea enjoy a tradition of snacking on appetizer-size dishes based on fresh, local ingredients. Start your own meal with dishes called "tapas" in Spain, "hors d'oeuvres" in France, "antipasti" in Italy or "mezes" in Greece. The first courses in this chapter are designed to whet the appetite but sometimes they become a meal in themselves. Marinated Olives (recipe, page 15), Spicy Spanish Walnuts, Meze Platter (recipes, page 14)

Spicy SPANish WALNuts

2 Tbsp. butter *or* margarine

3 Tbsp. sugar

2 tsp. *each* grated orange peel *and* lime peel

1 tsp. *each* ground coriander, ground cinnamon *and* ground cloves

¼ tsp. *each* ground red pepper *and* salt

2 cups California walnut halves

MELT butter in medium saucepan on low heat. Add sugar, peels and spices.

TOSS walnuts with spice mixture. Spoon onto cookie sheet.

BAKE at 300°F for 20 minutes or until walnuts are toasted, stirring every 5 minutes. Cool. Makes 2 cups.

Prep time: 10 minutes
Baking time: 20 minutes

Photo, pages 12–13.

meze Platter

Assorted grilled vegetables (such as zucchini pieces, thinly sliced potatoes, eggplant *and* roasted red pepper strips)

Assorted ATHENOS Mediterranean Spreads (Hummus, 3-Pepper Hummus, Whipped Feta Spread *and* Whipped Feta Spread with Tomato & Basil)

Marinated Olives (recipe opposite)

Pita bread, cut into triangles

ARRANGE vegetables, spreads, olives and pita triangles on large serving platter. Garnish with fresh herbs, if desired.

Prep time: 20 to 30 minutes (for grilling vegetables)

Photo, pages 12–13.

A meze (meh-ZAY) is a Greek or Middle Eastern appetizer. It's often accompanied by beer, wine or the strong, anise-flavored liqueur, ouzo, in some Greek tavernas.

California Ripe Olives take on a world of flavors when they're marinated in olive oil infused with fragrant herbs.

Marinated Olives

1 can (6 oz.) pitted California ripe olives, drained

Seasonings (see right)

MIX 1 can of olives and seasonings. Refrigerate 2 hours or overnight. Makes 1¾ cups.

Seasonings

Greek: 2 Tbsp. COLAVITA Extra Virgin Olive Oil, 1 Tbsp. *each* fresh lemon juice *and* COLAVITA Red Wine Vinegar and 1 tsp. dried oregano leaves.

Italian: 2 Tbsp. COLAVITA Extra Virgin Olive Oil, 1 clove garlic, minced, ½ tsp. dried basil leaves and ¼ tsp. crushed red pepper.

Spanish: 2 Tbsp. COLAVITA Extra Virgin Olive Oil, 1 Tbsp. COLAVITA Red Wine Vinegar, 1 clove garlic, minced, 2 tsp. finely chopped chives and ¼ tsp. *each* ground red pepper *and* paprika.

French: 2 Tbsp. COLAVITA Extra Virgin Olive Oil and 2 cloves garlic, minced.

Prep time: 5 minutes plus refrigerating

Photo, pages 12–13. Pictured with cubes of ATHENOS feta cheese.

Olive & Onion Focaccia

1 prepared Basic Pizza Dough
   (recipe, page 18)

¼ cup **COLAVITA Extra Virgin
   Olive Oil**

3 cups sliced onions

1 tsp. dried rosemary leaves

1 can (2½ oz.) sliced California
   ripe olives, drained

   Salt *and* pepper

Focaccia (foh-KAH-chee-uh) is an Italian flat bread. This mouthwatering version is made with the same dough used for pizza on page 18.

SPRAY cookie sheet with no stick cooking spray. Stretch dough to 11-inch circle; transfer to prepared cookie sheet. Bake at 350°F for 15 minutes.

HEAT oil in large skillet. Add onions and rosemary; cook and stir on medium heat 12 minutes or until onions are tender and golden brown.

SPREAD onions over crust. Top with olives. Sprinkle with salt and pepper to taste. Bake at 350°F for 20 to 25 minutes or until crust is golden brown. Let cool 5 minutes. Transfer to cutting board. Cut into squares or wedges to serve. Makes 12 servings.

Variation: Substitute 1 can (10 oz.) refrigerated pizza dough for Basic Pizza Dough. Spray 15x10x1-inch baking pan with no stick cooking spray. Press dough into prepared pan. Bake at 425°F for 5 to 7 minutes or until lightly browned. Top as directed with onions and olives. Sprinkle with pepper. Bake 5 minutes or until crust is golden brown. Let cool in pan 5 minutes. Cut and serve as directed.

Prep time: 20 minutes
Baking time: 40 minutes plus cooling

Basic Pizza Dough

1 cup lukewarm (108°F) water
1 pkg. quick-rise yeast
1 Tbsp. COLAVITA Extra Virgin Olive Oil
2¾ cups bread flour
1 tsp. salt

POUR water over yeast in small bowl. Let stand 5 minutes to soften. Add oil.

PLACE flour and salt in food processor container fitted with steel blade; cover. Pulse 2 or 3 times to mix. Add the softened yeast mixture.

PROCESS 1 minute (dough will form into ball and move around workbowl). Stop processing. Divide dough in 3 pieces and return all 3 pieces to workbowl. Process 1 minute longer. Remove from processor and place in greased bowl to raise, covered with towel, 30 minutes. Proceed as directed in recipe.

To make ahead: After dough has risen, punch down, shape into a ball and wrap with freezer wrap. Freeze. To use dough, thaw in a greased bowl covered with a towel at room temperature several hours or until double.

Manual method: Soften yeast as directed. Add oil. Mix flour and salt in large bowl, making a well in the middle. Pour in yeast mixture. Mix until soft dough forms. Transfer to floured board. Knead until smooth and no longer sticky, adding more flour if necessary. Raise as directed.

Prep time: 10 minutes plus raising

Simply whirl the ingredients in your food processor for a base that's perfect for any topping. It's easy to make by hand, too! Try using the dough in the recipe for Olive & Onion Focaccia on page 17.

Choose either DI GIORNO Grated or Shredded Romano Cheese to top this easy pizza made with a prebaked crust. Using grated or shredded cheese spreads the cheese's robust flavor over an entire dish.

PIZZA ROMANA

1   Italian bread shell (12 inch)
1   Tbsp. COLAVITA Extra Virgin Olive Oil
½   cup (2 oz.) DI GIORNO Grated *or* Shredded Romano Cheese, divided
3   plum tomatoes, sliced
¼   tsp. ground black pepper
2   Tbsp. shredded fresh basil leaves

Plum Tomatoes

BRUSH bread shell with oil.

SPRINKLE ¼ cup of the cheese over crust. Top with tomato slices and remaining ¼ cup cheese. Sprinkle with pepper.

BAKE directly on oven rack at 450°F for 8 to 10 minutes or until crust is crisp and cheese is melted. Sprinkle with basil before serving. Makes 4 to 6 servings.

Variation: Substitute DI GIORNO Parmesan *or* Pecorino Romano Cheese for DI GIORNO Romano Cheese.

Variation: Substitute ½ of prepared Basic Pizza Dough (recipe, opposite page) for Italian bread shell (freeze remaining half of dough). Spray 12-inch pizza pan with no stick cooking spray; dust with cornmeal. Roll dough on lightly floured surface to 13-inch circle. Place in prepared pan, pushing overhanging dough back to sides of pan to create edge. Top pizza as directed. Bake at 400°F for 15 to 16 minutes or until crust is golden brown. Sprinkle with basil as directed.

Prep time: 5 minutes
Baking time: 10 minutes

Torta (TOHR-tuh) means cake in Italian or Spanish. This version looks like a cake but is really a hearty appetizer. Cut it into wedges and serve warm or at room temperature.

- **1 pkg. (17¼ oz.) frozen puff pastry, thawed, divided**
- **4 eggs**
- **2 pkg. (10 oz. each) frozen chopped spinach, thawed, squeezed dry**
- **2 cups (8 oz.) shredded natural mozzarella cheese**
- **1 cup ricotta cheese**
- **1 pkg. (8 oz.) ATHENOS Feta Cheese, crumbled**
- **¾ cup (3 oz.) DI GIORNO Shredded Parmesan Cheese**
- **½ cup dry bread crumbs**
- **½ cup chopped onion**
- **1 jar (12 oz.) roasted red peppers, drained, sliced**
- **1 egg, beaten**

ROLL 1 puff pastry sheet into 16-inch circle on lightly floured surface. Press onto bottom and sides of 9-inch springform pan sprayed with no stick cooking spray, leaving 2-inch overhang.

MIX 4 eggs, spinach, cheeses, bread crumbs and onion. Spoon ½ of the cheese mixture into prepared pan. Top with peppers and remaining cheese mixture.

ROLL remaining puff pastry sheet on lightly floured surface; cut out 9-inch circle. Place over filling, pinching edges to seal. Cut remaining pastry into cutouts, if desired. Place on top of crust. Brush top of crust with remaining beaten egg. Place pan on cookie sheet.

BAKE at 425°F for 40 minutes or until golden brown. Cool 30 minutes. Run knife along edges and carefully remove pan. Serve warm or at room temperature. Makes 10 servings.

Prep time: 20 minutes
Baking time: 40 minutes
Cooling time: 30 minutes

TORTA RUSTICA

Sicilian Garbanzos

2 **Tbsp. COLAVITA Extra Virgin Olive Oil** *plus* **additional oil for drizzling**

1 **medium onion, chopped**

2 **cloves garlic, minced**

2 **cans (15 oz. each) garbanzo beans (chickpeas), rinsed, drained**

2 **plum tomatoes, seeded, chopped**

¼ **cup shredded fresh basil leaves**

½ **cup (2 oz.) DI GIORNO Shredded Parmesan Cheese**

¼ **tsp. ground black pepper**

HEAT 2 Tbsp. oil in large skillet. Add onion and garlic; cook and stir 5 minutes or until onion is tender.

ADD beans to skillet. Cook and stir 5 minutes or until thoroughly heated. Transfer to serving platter.

TOP with tomatoes and basil. Just before serving, drizzle with olive oil; toss with cheese. Sprinkle with pepper. Serve warm or at room temperature. Makes 4 to 6 servings.

Note: As a condiment, COLAVITA Extra Virgin Olive Oil is perfect for drizzling, brushing over garlic bread before toasting or just plain dipping.

Prep time: 10 minutes
Cooking time: 10 minutes

For a light lunch, why not make this Italian dish the star of an antipasto tray? Just add a variety of cold cuts, cheese cubes, olives, pickled peppers and some marinated artichoke hearts.

Hot & Spicy Artichoke Dip

- 1 can (14 oz.) artichoke hearts, drained, chopped
- 1 cup KRAFT Mayo Real Mayonnaise
- 1 cup (4 oz.) DI GIORNO Grated Parmesan Cheese
- 1 can (4 oz.) chopped green chilies, drained
- 1 clove garlic, minced
- 2 Tbsp. chopped California ripe olives
- 2 Tbsp. chopped seeded tomato

MIX all ingredients except olives and tomato until blended. Spoon into shallow ovenproof dish or 9-inch pie plate.

BAKE at 350°F for 20 to 25 minutes or until lightly browned. Sprinkle with olives and tomato.

SERVE with crackers or toasted pita bread wedges. Makes 2 cups.

Prep time: 10 minutes
Baking time: 25 minutes

Mediterranean Quesadillas

- 12 flour tortillas (6 inch)
  COLAVITA Extra Virgin Olive Oil
- 4 oz. (½ of 8 oz. pkg.) ATHENOS Feta Cheese, finely chopped
- 1½ cups (2 oz.) lightly packed fresh basil leaves
- 1 cup thinly sliced roasted red pepper strips (54 strips)
- ¼ cup chopped California ripe olives

BRUSH 1 side of 6 of the tortillas lightly with oil. Turn tortillas over; sprinkle entire surface of each with 2 Tbsp. feta cheese. Top each with about 6 to 9 basil leaves, 9 pepper strips and 2 tsp. olives. Cover with second flour tortilla; brush top lightly with oil.

COOK in batches in large skillet on medium heat 2 to 3 minutes on each side or until lightly browned. Cut each into 6 wedges. Makes 3 dozen appetizers.

Prep time: 15 minutes
Cooking time: 6 minutes per batch

Mediterranean Meat Balls with Yogurt & Feta Sauce

Meatballs
- 1 lb. ground beef
- ½ cup chopped, fresh, flat leaf parsley
- 1 egg
- ¼ cup dry bread crumbs
- 2 cloves garlic, minced
- ½ tsp. salt
- ¼ tsp. ground black pepper
- 1 Tbsp. COLAVITA Extra Virgin Olive Oil

Sauce
- 1 pkg. (4 oz.) ATHENOS Crumbled Feta Cheese
- ¾ cup plain lowfat yogurt
- 2 Tbsp. milk
- 1 clove garlic, peeled
- ⅓ cup *each* chopped seeded tomato *and* chopped, seeded and peeled cucumber
- 1 tsp. finely chopped fresh dill

MIX meat, parsley, egg, crumbs, garlic, salt and pepper for meatballs. Shape into 1-inch meatballs.

HEAT oil in medium skillet. Add meatballs. Cook on medium-low heat 12 to 15 minutes or until cooked through, stirring occasionally.

PLACE cheese, yogurt, milk and garlic for sauce in food processor container fitted with steel blade or in blender container; cover. Blend until smooth.

STIR in tomato, cucumber and dill. Garnish with dill sprig, if desired. Serve sauce with meatballs. Makes 20 meatballs and 2 cups sauce.

Variation: Substitute ground lamb for half or all of the beef.

Note: For a main-dish sandwich, serve the meatballs and feta-yogurt sauce tucked inside warm pita bread halves.

Prep time: 15 minutes
Cooking time: 15 minutes

Feta cheese, the major ingredient of the meatball dipping sauce, is a semisoft, white cheese with a distinctively Mediterranean flavor. The taste of feta is a perfect complement to meatballs, which are familiar taverna fare.

MIX feta cheese and cream cheese with electric mixer on medium speed until well blended. Add walnuts, onions and red pepper; mix well. Refrigerate.

SHAPE into ball. Roll in additional chopped walnuts or chopped fresh parsley, if desired. Serve with assorted crackers. Makes 4 cups.

Cheese Mold: Prepare the cheese mixture as directed. Line 4-cup mold with plastic wrap; lightly spray with no stick cooking spray. Sprinkle with chopped fresh parsley. Fill mold with cheese mixture. Refrigerate. Just before serving, unmold onto serving plate; remove plastic wrap. Garnish as desired.

Note: For smaller molds, recipe may be halved.

Cheese Wreath: Prepare the cheese mixture as directed. Refrigerate several hours. Place drinking glass, about 3 inches in diameter, in center of serving platter. Drop rounded tablespoonfuls of mixture around glass, just touching outer edge of glass to form ring; smooth with spatula. Remove glass. Garnish with chopped fresh parsley and red bell pepper.

Prep time: 15 minutes plus refrigerating

- **2 pkg. (8 oz. each) ATHENOS Feta Cheese, coarsely chopped**
- **2 pkg. (8 oz. each) PHILADELPHIA BRAND Cream Cheese, softened**
- **1 cup chopped California walnuts**
- **¼ cup *each* sliced green onions *and* finely chopped red pepper**

Feta Cheese Ball

Refrigerate shelled California walnuts in a tightly covered container for up to 6 months. For longer storage, keep the shelled nuts in the freezer. Store unshelled walnuts in a cool, dry place up to 6 months.

This intensely flavored olive spread, tapenade (ta-pen-AHD), hails from the Provence region of France, where there may be as many tapenade versions as there are cooks. Serve the spread with crackers or toasted French bread slices for an appetizer or light snack.

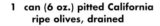

BlAck Olive Tapenade

1 can (6 oz.) pitted California ripe olives, drained
2 Tbsp. COLAVITA Extra Virgin Olive Oil
2 Tbsp. drained capers
2 cloves garlic, peeled
2 anchovies
¼ tsp. ground black pepper

PLACE all ingredients in food processor container fitted with steel blade; cover.

PROCESS until finely chopped, scraping down sides of container once or twice. Serve with crackers or toasted French bread. Makes 1½ cups.

Manual method: Finely chop olives, capers, garlic and anchovies. Add olive oil and pepper; mix well. Serve spread as directed.

Prep time: 5 minutes

Put together this simple appetizer and begin your Mediterranean cooking experience. It takes little effort to assemble and uses just a few ingredients.

Pita bread, split

COLAVITA Extra Virgin Olive Oil

ATHENOS Mediterranean Spreads (Hummus *and* 3-Pepper Hummus)

Thinly sliced green onions *and* shredded carrots

Sliced California ripe olives

BRUSH cut side of pita bread rounds with oil. Place on cookie sheet. Broil 1 minute or until crisp.

SPREAD each pita bread round with 2 Tbsp. hummus.

SPRINKLE with vegetables. Cut each pita bread round into 4 wedges to serve.

Note: Hummus is a distinctive spread of mashed garbanzo beans. Although a famous Middle Eastern dish, hummus has found a prominent place on tables this side of the Atlantic, too. ATHENOS Mediterranean Spreads offer a variety of hummus flavors that allow you to customize this appetizer to suit your individual tastes.

Prep time: 10 minutes

Hummus & Vegetable Pita Toasts

GRAINS, Rice

& Pasta

Bulgur, rice, couscous and pasta—these are the staples that the people of the Mediterranean basin have been cooking and thriving on for centuries. Here, these stars of the Mediterranean kitchen are spotlighted in both contemporary fare and in some of the most mouth-watering classics of the region.

Garden Tabbouleh (recipe, page 32)

gARden TABBouleh

Traditionally, tabbouleh, a Lebanese salad made with bulgur, is served with crisp lettuce leaves, which are used to scoop up the lemony mixture. Look for bulgur, a wheat product, near rice and other grains in the supermarket.

1 cup bulgur

1½ cups boiling water

¼ cup COLAVITA Extra Virgin Olive Oil

2 to 3 Tbsp. fresh lemon juice (see note, page 51)

1 clove garlic, minced

½ tsp. dried mint flakes

½ tsp. salt

1 pkg. (4 oz.) ATHENOS Crumbled Feta Cheese *or* Feta Cheese with Peppercorn

1 cup chopped fresh parsley

1 tomato, chopped

½ cup chopped green onions

MIX bulgur and boiling water; cover. Let stand 20 minutes or until bulgur is soft.

STIR in oil, juice, garlic, mint and salt.

ADD remaining ingredients; mix lightly. Garnish with fresh mint leaves, if desired. Makes 10 servings.

Prep time: 25 minutes

Photo, pages 30–31.

In North Africa, making couscous by hand is a tradition handed down from mother to daughter. The uncooked granules are steamed in the top of a two-tiered apparatus known as a couscoussier. This recipe, adapted to the American kitchen, is much easier to make.

Spicy Vegetable Couscous

- 1 can (13¾ oz.) chicken broth
- 1 cup couscous
- 2 Tbsp. COLAVITA Extra Virgin Olive Oil
- 1 cup *each* chopped zucchini *and* red onion
- ½ cup grated carrots
- 1 clove garlic, minced
- 1 can (19 oz.) garbanzo beans (chickpeas), rinsed, drained
- ½ tsp. *each* ground cumin, curry powder, salt *and* red pepper flakes

BRING broth to a boil. Stir in couscous. Remove from heat. Let stand, covered, 5 minutes.

HEAT oil in large skillet. Add zucchini, onion, carrots and garlic; cook and stir 5 minutes or until tender.

ADD beans, seasonings and couscous; cook and stir until thoroughly heated, about 2 minutes. Makes 6 servings.

Prep time: 15 minutes
Cooking time: 12 minutes plus standing

Photo, page 73.

Garbanzo Beans

This unique side dish consists of rice that gains flavor through being sautéed before it's simmered in broth. Crumbled feta cheese with peppercorns and oregano add a Greek flair.

3 Tbsp. COLAVITA Extra Virgin Olive Oil

⅓ cup finely chopped onion

1½ cups long grain rice, uncooked

1 can (13¾ oz.) chicken broth

¾ cup water

6 oz. ATHENOS Feta Cheese with Peppercorn, crumbled

2 Tbsp. chopped fresh oregano or 2 tsp. dried oregano leaves

HEAT oil in medium saucepan. Add onion; cook and stir 3 to 4 minutes or until tender. Add rice; cook and stir 1 minute.

STIR in broth and water. Bring to a boil. Reduce heat to low; cover. Simmer 15 minutes or until liquid is absorbed.

STIR in cheese and oregano. Garnish with fresh herbs, if desired. Makes 4 servings.

Variation: Omit oregano. Stir in 2 Tbsp. chopped fresh mint.

Prep time: 5 minutes
Cooking time: 20 minutes

grecian Rice

Quick & Easy Risotto

- **2 Tbsp. COLAVITA Extra Virgin Olive Oil**
- **1 cup chopped mushrooms**
- **1/3 cup sliced green onions**
- **1 cup long grain rice, uncooked**
- **1 1/2 cups water**
- **1/2 cup dry white wine**
- **3/4 cup (3 oz.) DI GIORNO Shredded Pecorino Romano Cheese, divided**
- **1/4 cup half-and-half or milk**

HEAT oil in saucepan. Add mushrooms and onions; cook and stir on medium heat 5 minutes or until tender.

STIR in rice, water and wine. Bring to a boil. Reduce heat to low; cover. Simmer 20 minutes or until rice is tender.

STIR in 1/2 cup of the cheese and half-and-half. Serve with remaining cheese. Makes 4 to 6 servings.

Prep time: 10 minutes
Cooking time: 25 minutes

Photo, page 75.

Pasta with Olive Pesto

- **8 oz. pasta (such as mafalda or radiatore)**
- **1 1/2 cups pitted California ripe olives**
- **1/4 cup COLAVITA Extra Virgin Olive Oil**
- **4 tsp. lemon juice**
- **2 cloves garlic, peeled**
- **1/2 cup finely chopped fresh basil leaves**
- **1/2 cup (2 oz.) DI GIORNO Grated Parmesan Cheese**

COOK pasta as package directs; drain.

PLACE olives, oil, juice and garlic in food processor container fitted with steel blade; cover. Process until coarsely pureed. Stir in remaining ingredients.

TOSS hot drained pasta with olive pesto. Sprinkle with additional cheese, if desired. Makes 4 servings.

Manual method: Finely chop olives and garlic. Mix olives, oil, juice, garlic, basil and cheese in medium bowl. Toss with hot drained pasta as directed.

Prep time: 15 minutes
Cooking time: 15 minutes

Mostaccioli with Spinach & Feta

- **8** oz. mostaccioli *or* penne pasta
- **2** Tbsp. COLAVITA Extra Virgin Olive Oil
- **3** cups chopped tomatoes
- **1** pkg. (10 oz.) fresh spinach, stems removed
- **½** cup chopped green onions
- **1** clove garlic, minced
- **1** pkg. (8 oz.) ATHENOS Feta Cheese with Basil & Tomato, crumbled

COOK pasta as package directs; drain.

HEAT oil in same pan. Add tomatoes, spinach, onions and garlic; cook and stir 2 minutes or until spinach is wilted and mixture is thoroughly heated.

ADD pasta and cheese; cook 1 minute. Season to taste with salt and pepper, if desired. Makes 6 servings.

Prep time: 20 minutes
Cooking time: 15 minutes

Photo on the cover.

Mostaccioli (mos-tah-chee-OH-lee) and penne (PEN-nay) are both tubular-shaped pastas that partner perfectly with cooked vegetables and crumbled feta cheese.

You'll find that Romano cheese has a sharper and more robust flavor than Parmesan. Pair this flavorful cheese with California walnuts for a uniquely rich, nutty flavor. To save time in the kitchen, purchase cheese that has already been shredded.

Pasta with Creamy Garlic & Walnut Sauce

1½ cups heavy cream
1 cup California walnut halves, toasted, cooled (see note, page 55)
¾ cup (3 oz.) DI GIORNO Shredded Romano Cheese
3 cloves garlic, peeled
1 tsp. salt
½ tsp. ground black pepper
1 lb. shaped pasta (such as medium bow ties)

PLACE cream, walnuts, cheese, garlic, salt and pepper in food processor container fitted with steel blade; cover. Process until mixture is smooth.

COOK pasta as package directs; drain. Toss with sauce. Garnish with additional toasted walnuts and fresh herbs and serve immediately with additional cheese, if desired. Makes 6 servings.

Manual method: Finely grind cooled walnuts. Finely mince garlic. Mix cream, walnuts, cheese, garlic, salt and pepper. Continue as directed.

Note: When adding California walnuts to your Mediterranean dishes, you add texture and a great nutty taste as well.

Prep time: 10 minutes
Cooking time: 15 minutes

Fettuccine AL feta

12 oz. fettuccine

3 Tbsp. COLAVITA Extra Virgin Olive Oil

1 pkg. (8 oz.) ATHENOS Feta Cheese with Basil & Tomato, crumbled

2 cups chopped tomatoes

¼ cup julienne-cut fresh basil *or* 2 tsp. dried basil leaves

Ground black pepper

Salt

COOK fettuccine 8 to 10 minutes or until al dente. Drain. Return to pan; toss with oil.

TOSS with cheese, tomatoes and basil. Season to taste with pepper and salt. Makes 6 servings.

Variation: Substitute ATHENOS Feta Cheese with Garlic & Herb for ATHENOS Feta Cheese with Basil & Tomato.

Prep time: 10 minutes
Cooking time: 10 minutes

The Italian phrase "al dente" (ahl-DEN-tay) is a term used to describe perfectly cooked pasta. It literally means "to the tooth." Pasta should be tender when bitten, but still firm, so start testing for doneness at the minimum cooking time.

Mediterranean PAsta SAlad

1 lb. penne pasta

1 pkg. (8 oz.) ATHENOS Feta Cheese, crumbled

1 jar (6½ oz.) marinated artichoke hearts, drained, coarsely chopped

1 medium cucumber, seeded, chopped

1 small red onion, chopped

½ cup sun-dried tomato halves, cut into strips

¾ cup Italian dressing with red wine vinegar *or* Mediterranean Vinaigrette (recipe, page 47)

COOK pasta as package directs; drain.

MIX all ingredients lightly with dressing in large bowl. Serve immediately. Makes 8 servings.

Prep time: 20 minutes

There are several types of pecorino (peh-kuh-REE-noh), a cheese made from sheep's milk. Regional varieties are found in different parts of Italy—pecorino romano (in Rome), pecorino toscano (in Tuscany), and pecorino sardo (in Sardinia).

PEPPERY PECORINO PASTA

- **8 oz. ziti *or* rigatoni pasta**
- **¼ cup COLAVITA Extra Virgin Olive Oil**
- **1 cup (4 oz.) DI GIORNO Grated Pecorino Romano Cheese**
- **¼ tsp. *each* ground black pepper *and* red pepper flakes**

COOK pasta as package directs; drain.

HEAT oil in same pan. Toss cooked pasta in oil with cheese and peppers. Serve immediately. Makes 4 servings.

Prep time: 5 minutes
Cooking time: 15 minutes

Serve these eye-catching, cheese-filled shells in a trio for a main dish. Or, serve them by the dozen as an appetizer at your next get-together.

1 pkg. (10 oz.) frozen chopped spinach, thawed, well drained *or* 1 pkg. (10 oz.) fresh spinach, stems removed, cooked, well drained

1 cup ricotta cheese

1 pkg. (8 oz.) ATHENOS Feta Cheese, crumbled, divided

¼ tsp. garlic powder

12 jumbo macaroni shells, cooked, drained

1½ cups marinara sauce (see note, page 77)

MIX spinach, ricotta cheese, 6 oz. of the feta cheese and garlic powder in bowl.

FILL shells with spinach mixture. Place in 2-quart square or rectangular baking dish. Pour sauce over shells. Top with remaining 2 oz. feta cheese.

BAKE at 350°F for 20 minutes. Serve with mixed green salad and garnish with fresh herbs, if desired. Makes 4 servings.

Prep time: 20 minutes
Baking time: 20 minutes

Savory Feta-Filled Shells

SALADS &

With their piles of plump, ripe tomatoes, glossy eggplants and colorful bell peppers, fruit and vegetable markets in the Mediterranean are a glorious sight. It is because of this abundant variety that vegetables and salads make up a large part of the daily Mediterranean diet. In fact, they often are the centerpiece of the meal. Tomato & Orange Salad with Feta (recipe, page 46).

vegetables

Olive oil should be stored in a cool, dark place where it will stay fresh for up to a year. If you store olive oil in the refrigerator, let it stand at room temperature 10 to 15 minutes before using because it will be too thick to pour immediately.

Tomato & Orange Salad with Feta

Dressing

- ¼ cup COLAVITA Extra Virgin Olive Oil
- 1 Tbsp. COLAVITA Balsamic Vinegar
- ¼ tsp. *each* salt *and* pepper

Salad

- 4 large tomatoes, sliced ¼ inch thick
- 4 oranges, peeled, sliced ¼ inch thick
- 1 pkg. (8 oz.) ATHENOS Feta Cheese, sliced ⅛ inch thick
- ⅔ cup lightly packed small fresh basil leaves *or* 8 large fresh basil leaves, julienne-cut

MIX oil, vinegar and seasonings for dressing.

ARRANGE tomatoes, oranges and cheese alternately in overlapping circles on serving platter. Sprinkle with basil. Spoon dressing over salad. Makes 8 servings.

Prep time: 15 minutes

Photo, pages 44–45.

Mediterranean Potato Salad

- 2 lb. small red potatoes, quartered
- 1 pkg. (8 oz.) ATHENOS Feta Cheese with Garlic & Herb, crumbled
- 1 medium red pepper, chopped
- 1 medium cucumber, peeled, seeded, chopped
- ⅔ cup Italian dressing *or* Mediterranean Vinaigrette (recipe, below)
- ½ cup sliced green onions

COOK potatoes in boiling water 15 minutes or until just tender. Drain.

TOSS potatoes with remaining ingredients. Refrigerate. Stir before serving. Makes 8 servings.

Prep time: 15 minutes plus refrigerating
Cooking time: 15 minutes

When you want potatoes to keep their shape when cooked, choose a waxy type, such as round reds. They have a moist, smooth texture that is great for potato salads.

Mediterranean Vinaigrette

- 3 Tbsp. COLAVITA Red Wine Vinegar
- 2 cloves garlic, peeled
- 2 tsp. sugar
- 1 tsp. Dijon mustard
- ¾ tsp. salt
- ¼ tsp. ground black pepper
- ⅔ cup COLAVITA Extra Virgin Olive Oil

PLACE vinegar, garlic, sugar, mustard, salt and pepper in blender container; cover. Blend until smooth.

ADD oil. Blend 15 seconds or until well mixed and slightly opaque. Serve over fresh salad greens or in recipes calling for prepared dressings. Makes ¾ cup.

Prep time: 5 minutes

Tatziki (tot-ZEE-kee), a Greek dish, is sometimes served as an appetizer. The only change required is chopping the cucumbers. Serve the appetizer version with pita chips for scooping.

Feta Tatziki Salad

- 1 container (8 oz.) plain lowfat yogurt
- 1 pkg. (8 oz.) ATHENOS Feta Cheese, crumbled
- 1 clove garlic, peeled
- ½ tsp. salt
- 2 medium cucumbers, peeled, seeded, thinly sliced
- 1 tsp. chopped fresh mint *or* dried mint flakes (optional)

PLACE yogurt, cheese, garlic and salt in food processor container fitted with steel blade; cover. Process until smooth and creamy.

STIR in cucumbers. Sprinkle with mint. Makes 6 servings.

Mixer method: Mince garlic. Mix yogurt, cheese, garlic and salt in medium bowl with electric mixer until smooth and creamy. Stir in cucumbers. Sprinkle with mint.

Prep time: 10 minutes

White Bean & Tuna Salad

- 1 can (19 oz.) cannellini beans, rinsed, drained
- 1 can (6 oz.) solid white tuna packed in water, drained, flaked
- 2 Tbsp. sliced green onion
- 2 Tbsp. COLAVITA Extra Virgin Olive Oil
- 1 Tbsp. COLAVITA Balsamic Vinegar
- 1 clove garlic, minced

MIX all ingredients. Refrigerate.

SERVE with crusty Italian or toasted pita bread. Makes 4 servings.

Prep time: 10 minutes plus refrigerating

SMoked TURKey & FEta SALAD

- 1 lb. asparagus spears, cut into 2-inch pieces, cooked, drained
- 1 pkg. (6 oz.) smoked turkey breast slices, cut into strips
- 1 red pepper, cut into strips
- 1 pkg. (4 oz.) ATHENOS Crumbled Feta Cheese
- ½ cup thinly sliced red onion
- ½ cup Italian dressing *or* Mediterranean Vinaigrette (recipe, page 47)

MIX all ingredients lightly with dressing. Refrigerate 2 hours.

SERVE on lettuce-lined platter, if desired. Makes 6 servings.

Prep time: 25 minutes plus refrigerating

When preparing fresh asparagus, break off and discard the woody bases where the spears snap easily. Cut asparagus into pieces and cook, covered, in a small amount of boiling salted water until crisp-tender, about 4 to 6 minutes.

asparagus

Greek chefs often prepare this salad with garden-fresh vegetables. As in Greece, this version is simply dressed with olive oil, a touch of lemon juice and seasonings.

ATHENOS Greek Salad

Dressing

½ cup COLAVITA Extra Virgin Olive Oil

¼ cup fresh lemon juice

1 clove garlic, minced

1 tsp. dried oregano leaves

½ tsp. salt (or to taste)

¼ tsp. ground black pepper

Salad

1 pkg. (10 oz.) salad greens

1 cup pitted California ripe olives *or* Greek olives

3 plum tomatoes, cut into chunks

½ cup thinly sliced red onion

½ medium cucumber, peeled, cut into chunks

1 pkg. (4 oz.) ATHENOS Crumbled Feta Cheese

MIX oil, juice, garlic and seasonings for dressing.

TOSS greens, olives, tomatoes, onion and cucumber for salad. Toss with dressing. Spoon onto serving platter.

SPRINKLE with cheese. Makes 6 servings.

Variation: Substitute ⅔ cup Mediterranean Vinaigrette (recipe, page 47) *or* ⅔ cup Italian dressing for dressing mixture.

Note: One large lemon, squeezed, will yield about ¼ cup fresh lemon juice.

Prep time: 10 minutes

Deep-green spinach, golden melon chunks, ruby strawberries and red onion rings star in this colorful side dish. Top with feta, olives and a honey-lemon dressing for a fresh-tasting Mediterranean salad.

Dressing

- ¼ cup **COLAVITA Extra Virgin Olive Oil**
- ¼ cup **fresh lemon juice (see note, page 51)**
- 2 tsp. **honey**
- ¼ tsp. **ground black pepper**

Salad

- 5 cups **torn spinach**
- 1 cup *each* **cantaloupe chunks** *and* **halved strawberries**
- 1 cup (6 oz.) **crumbled ATHENOS Feta Cheese**
- ½ cup **thinly sliced red onion, separated into rings**
- ¼ cup **pitted California ripe olives**

MIX oil, juice, honey and pepper for dressing in small bowl.

TOSS spinach, fruit, cheese, onion and olives for salad in large bowl. Spoon dressing over spinach mixture. Makes 6 servings.

Prep time: 15 minutes

SpiNach, FRuit & Feta SALad

Rustic Bread Salad

½ lb. day-old Italian bread, torn into chunks

3 cups ripe tomato chunks

¾ cup thinly sliced red onion rings, cut in half

½ cup (2 oz.) DI GIORNO Shredded Parmesan Cheese

⅓ cup pitted California ripe olives, cut in half lengthwise

¾ cup Italian dressing *or* Mediterranean Vinaigrette (recipe, page 47)

PLACE bread chunks in bottom of salad bowl.

TOSS tomato, onion, cheese and olives; place over bread.

POUR dressing over salad just before serving; toss lightly. Makes 6 to 8 servings.

Variation: Substitute DI GIORNO Romano *or* Pecorino Romano Cheese for DI GIORNO Parmesan Cheese.

Note: DI GIORNO Shredded Parmesan Cheese is the perfect ingredient for this hearty salad. Store the shredded cheese in the refrigerator.

Prep time: 20 minutes

Here's a simple and delicious salad that starts with day-old bread. Be sure the bread is crusty and heavy in texture. The recipe is reminiscent of the Italian classic, panzanella, which is usually made at the peak of the tomato season when the tomatoes are at their juicy best.

Your supermarket produce aisle is brimming with packaged mixed greens, ready to toss into salads. Try your favorite mixture with these roasted pepper, nut and feta embellishments. The feta cheese and walnuts add protein to the salad for a nutritious flavor boost.

Roasted Pepper Salad with Feta & Walnuts

6 cups torn mixed salad greens

1 jar (12 oz.) roasted red peppers, drained, cut into strips

1 small red onion, thinly sliced

1 cup California walnuts, toasted, chopped

½ cup red wine vinaigrette *or* Mediterranean Vinaigrette (recipe, page 47)

1 pkg. (4 oz.) ATHENOS Crumbled Feta Cheese

MIX greens, vegetables and walnuts.

TOSS lightly with vinaigrette. Spoon onto serving platter.

SPRINKLE with cheese. Makes 6 servings.

Note: Toast walnuts on cookie sheet at 400°F for 5 minutes or until lightly brown and fragrant.

Prep time: 15 minutes

Ratatouille

1 small eggplant, cut into ½-inch cubes

Salt

8 Tbsp. COLAVITA Extra Virgin Olive Oil, divided

2 large red peppers, cut into ¾-inch pieces

4 small zucchini, cut in half lengthwise, sliced

1 onion, coarsely chopped

4 cloves garlic, minced

1 lb. tomatoes, chopped *or* 1 can (28 oz.) whole tomatoes, drained, chopped

⅓ cup chopped fresh basil leaves

SPRINKLE eggplant with salt. Place salted eggplant in colander to drain for 30 minutes. Pat dry with paper towels.

HEAT 4 Tbsp. of the oil in large nonstick skillet. Add eggplant; cook and stir 6 to 7 minutes or until soft and brown. Push cooked eggplant to side of pan; add 3 Tbsp. of the oil, red peppers, zucchini, onion and garlic to center of pan. Cook and stir 3 to 5 minutes or until tender; push to side of pan. Add remaining 1 Tbsp. oil and tomatoes; cook and stir 3 minutes. Mix tomatoes and vegetables; cover. Cook on low heat 15 to 20 minutes or until vegetables are very tender, stirring occasionally.

STIR in basil. Garnish with additional fresh basil leaves, if desired. Makes 6 servings.

Variation: Stir in 2 Tbsp. dry red wine and ½ cup chopped California ripe olives with fresh basil.

Prep time: 35 minutes
Cooking time: 35 minutes

This vegetable specialty of the Provence region of France typically features eggplant and tomatoes. It's delicious served either hot or cold.

Lentil salads are served in almost every country of the Mediterranean. In France, the red pepper, mint and feta would be replaced with carrots, chives and goat cheese. An Italian version would add extra garlic and some parsley to the lentil mixture.

1 **cup dry lentils**
¾ **cup chopped red pepper**
⅓ **cup chopped red onion**
2 **Tbsp. chopped fresh mint (optional)**
6 **Tbsp. COLAVITA Extra Virgin Olive Oil**
6 **Tbsp. COLAVITA Balsamic Vinegar**
2 **cloves garlic, minced**
1 **pkg. (8 oz.) ATHENOS Feta Cheese, crumbled**

PLACE lentils in saucepan. Pour enough water into pan to cover lentils by 2 inches. Cook on medium heat 30 minutes or until tender. Drain. Transfer to a bowl. Add red pepper, onion and mint. Refrigerate until ready to serve.

MIX oil, vinegar and garlic. Pour over lentil mixture; mix ingredients lightly.

TOSS with cheese. Serve in red pepper quarters and garnish with additional fresh mint leaves, if desired. Makes 6 to 8 servings.

Prep time: 10 minutes plus refrigerating
Cooking time: 30 minutes

LeBANese LeNtils & Red Peppers

PAN-FRIED GREEK POTATOES

- **4** slices bacon, chopped
- **2** medium potatoes, very thinly sliced
- **¼** cup sliced green onions
- **1** pkg. (4 oz.) ATHENOS Crumbled Feta Cheese with Basil & Tomato

COOK and stir bacon in large nonstick skillet on medium-high heat until bacon is crisp. Remove bacon with slotted spoon to paper towels.

ADD potatoes to bacon drippings in pan. Cook on medium-low heat 15 minutes or until tender, stirring occasionally. Add onions; cook and stir 2 minutes. Remove from heat.

STIR in cheese. Serve immediately. Makes 4 servings.

Variation: Substitute ATHENOS Feta Cheese with Peppercorn for ATHENOS Feta with Basil & Tomato.

Prep time: 10 minutes
Cooking time: 25 minutes

Potatoes

Make quick work of chopping the raw bacon slices by using your kitchen scissors to snip the slices into small pieces.

This soup is one of the best-loved dishes in Italian cuisine. Versions all have one thing in common—they're rich in garden vegetables.

Hearty Minestrone

- 2 Tbsp. COLAVITA Extra Virgin Olive Oil
- 1 large potato, peeled, diced
- 2 cups shredded green cabbage
- 2 medium zucchini, diced
- 2 medium carrots, diced
- 1 medium onion, chopped
- 1 can (32 oz.) chicken broth
- 1 cup elbow macaroni, uncooked
- 1 can (19 oz.) cannellini beans rinsed, drained
- Ground black pepper
- DI GIORNO Shredded Pecorino Romano Cheese

HEAT oil in large saucepan. Add potato, cabbage, zucchini, carrots and onion. Cook and stir 8 to 10 minutes or until cabbage is wilted.

STIR in broth. Bring to a boil. Reduce heat to low; add macaroni. Cook 10 minutes or until macaroni is cooked and vegetables are tender.

ADD beans. Cook about 5 minutes or until beans are thoroughly heated. Season to taste with pepper. Sprinkle each serving generously with cheese. Makes 6 to 8 servings.

Prep time: 15 minutes
Cooking time: 25 minutes

Tomato-Basil Sauce

- 3 cloves garlic, minced
- ¼ cup COLAVITA Extra Virgin Olive Oil
- 1 can (28 oz.) crushed tomatoes in puree
- ½ cup chopped fresh parsley
- 8 fresh basil leaves, finely chopped
- ½ tsp. crushed red pepper flakes

COOK and stir garlic in oil in large skillet just until garlic turns golden.

STIR in remaining ingredients. Simmer 15 minutes or until sauce begins to thicken. Season to taste with salt. Serve over hot cooked pasta. Makes 6 servings (enough for 1 lb. pasta).

Note: Serve this spicy sauce with hot cooked pasta and DI GIORNO Grated or Shredded Parmesan, Romano or Pecorino Romano Cheese.

Prep time: 5 minutes
Cooking time: 20 minutes

Herb-Roasted Mediterranean Vegetables

8 cups assorted vegetable pieces (such as cubed eggplant, zucchini and onion, halved carrots, cut up peppers, *and* baby turnips)

¼ cup COLAVITA Extra Virgin Olive Oil

2 cloves garlic, minced

2 tsp. dried rosemary leaves

1 tsp. salt

½ cup (2 oz.) DI GIORNO Shredded Parmesan Cheese

TOSS vegetables with oil, garlic, rosemary and salt. Place in 15x10x1-inch baking pan.

BAKE at 375°F for 40 minutes or until vegetables are tender, stirring once or twice during cooking.

SPRINKLE with cheese. Makes 6 to 8 servings.

Prep time: 15 minutes
Baking time: 40 minutes

For the best flavor when oven-roasting, use top-quality natural ingredients such as fresh vegetables and COLAVITA Extra Virgin Olive Oil. Extra virgin oil is from the first pressing of olives.

SEAfood, POUltry & MEAts

No matter where you are in the Mediterranean, the sea is never far away. So it should come as no surprise that fish and seafood appear in abundance on Mediterranean tables. And while poultry and meat dishes have not always been a daily component of the Mediterranean diet, they are becoming more and more common. Zuppa di Pesce (recipe, page 66)

- ¼ cup COLAVITA Extra Virgin Olive Oil
- 1 medium onion, chopped
- 2 cloves garlic, minced
- 1 can (28 oz.) Italian-style plum tomatoes, undrained
- ½ cup dry white wine
- 2 Tbsp. julienne-cut fresh basil leaves
- 2 lb. soft-flesh fish fillets (such as cod, red snapper, orange roughy *or* a mixture), cut into chunks
  DI GIORNO Shredded Parmesan Cheese

HEAT oil in large saucepan. Add onion and garlic; cook and stir 4 to 5 minutes or until tender.

STIR in tomatoes, wine and basil, breaking up tomatoes with back of spoon. Bring to a boil. Reduce heat to medium-low; cook, uncovered, 10 minutes.

ADD fish. Simmer 10 minutes or until fish flakes easily with fork. Ladle into serving bowls. Sprinkle with cheese. Garnish with additional julienne-cut fresh basil leaves, if desired. Makes 4 to 6 servings.

Note: Parmesan is a very hard cheese made from cow's milk. It has a granular texture that when grated or shredded is very fine. It is a relatively low-fat cheese.

Prep time: 15 minutes
Cooking time: 25 minutes

Photo, pages 64–65.

Zuppa di Pesce

Zuppa di Pesce, fish soup, is popular on the island of Sicily. Serve it with a hearty bread to soak up the juices.

BAKed Fish
with Olive Relish

½ cup stuffed green olives, chopped

½ cup pitted California ripe olives

1 Tbsp. chopped fresh parsley

1 tsp. COLAVITA Red Wine Vinegar

1 clove garlic, minced

3 Tbsp. COLAVITA Extra Virgin Olive Oil, divided

4 halibut *or* swordfish steaks, 1 inch thick (about 1½ lb.)

Salt *and* pepper

MIX olives, parsley, vinegar, garlic and 1 Tbsp. of the oil.

ARRANGE fish in a 13x9-inch baking dish and brush with remaining 2 Tbsp. oil. Sprinkle with salt and pepper.

BAKE at 400°F for 20 to 25 minutes or until fish flakes easily with fork. Transfer to serving platter. Spoon olive mixture over fish. Makes 4 servings.

Note: Olive oil is very stable at high temperatures. Its smoke point is 437 degrees fahrenheit.

Prep time: 10 minutes
Baking time: 25 minutes

SHRIMP with Tomato & Feta

At seaside tavernas all over Greece, fish is prepared very simply—in understated marinades or uncomplicated sauces. The feta topping on this seafood main dish adds a finishing Mediterranean touch.

2 Tbsp. COLAVITA Extra Virgin Olive Oil

½ cup chopped onion

1 can (28 oz.) Italian-style plum tomatoes, drained, cut up

⅓ cup dry white wine

2 tsp. dried oregano leaves

12 oz. medium shrimp, cleaned

1 pkg. (4 oz.) ATHENOS Crumbled Feta Cheese

2 Tbsp. chopped fresh parsley

HEAT oil in large skillet. Add onion; cook and stir on medium heat 3 minutes. Add tomatoes, wine and oregano. Bring to a boil. Reduce heat to low; simmer, uncovered, 5 minutes or until thickened.

ADD shrimp. Cook 3 minutes, stirring frequently, until shrimp are pink.

SPRINKLE with cheese; simmer 1 minute. Stir in parsley. Serve with hot cooked rice and garnish with fresh herbs, if desired. Makes 4 servings.

Prep time: 20 minutes
Cooking time: 12 minutes

Chicken España

MIX olives, oil, vinegar, oregano and garlic. Pour over chicken in large zipper-style plastic bag; seal bag. Marinate in refrigerator 2 hours or overnight, turning occasionally.

ARRANGE chicken with marinade in shallow baking pan. Sprinkle with brown sugar. Pour wine into pan.

BAKE at 350°F for 1 hour or until cooked through, basting every 20 minutes. Sprinkle with parsley. Makes 4 to 6 servings.

Prep time: 10 minutes plus marinating
Baking time: 1 hour

½ cup pitted California ripe olives

¼ cup COLAVITA Extra Virgin Olive Oil

¼ cup COLAVITA Red Wine Vinegar

1 Tbsp. dried oregano leaves

3 cloves garlic, minced

1 broiler-fryer chicken, cut-up (3 to 3½ lb.)

¼ cup firmly packed brown sugar

¼ cup dry white wine

2 Tbsp. chopped fresh parsley

Mediterranean Chicken Breasts

½ cup (2 oz.) DI GIORNO Grated Pecorino Romano Cheese

¼ cup dry bread crumbs

1 tsp. dried basil leaves

¼ tsp. *each* paprika, salt *and* ground black pepper

6 boneless skinless chicken breast halves (about 2 lb.)

3 Tbsp. COLAVITA Extra Virgin Olive Oil

MIX cheese, crumbs and seasonings. Dip chicken in oil; coat with cheese mixture.

COOK chicken in skillet sprayed with no stick cooking spray on medium heat 5 to 7 minutes on each side or until cooked through. Makes 6 servings.

Prep time: 10 minutes
Cooking time: 14 minutes

Chicken & Pasta Toss

1 lb. bow tie pasta

3 cups broccoli flowerets

4 boneless skinless chicken breast halves (about 1¼ lb.), cooked, cut into strips

1 cup sun-dried tomatoes in olive oil

¼ cup olive oil from tomatoes

1½ cups (6 oz.) DI GIORNO Grated Romano Cheese

COOK pasta as package directs, adding broccoli to water during last 3 minutes cooking time. Drain pasta and broccoli.

TOSS pasta and broccoli with remaining ingredients. Season to taste with salt and pepper. Makes 4 to 6 servings.

Prep time: 15 minutes
Cooking time: 12 minutes

Adding the broccoli to the pasta as it cooks saves time as well as a cooking pan.

¾ cup Italian dressing *or* Mediterranean Vinaigrette (recipe, page 47)

1¼ lb. boneless skinless chicken breasts *or* beef tenderloin, cut into 1½-inch chunks

2 cups assorted vegetables (such as pepper chunks, zucchini slices *and* onion wedges)

POUR dressing over chicken and vegetables in large zipper-style plastic bag; seal bag. Marinate in refrigerator 2 hours or overnight, turning occasionally.

THREAD chicken and vegetables on 6 skewers.

GRILL over medium coals 5 to 7 minutes on each side or until cooked through. Serve with Spicy Vegetable Couscous (recipe, page 33) and garnish with fresh herbs, if desired. Makes 6 servings.

Note: If using wooden skewers, soak the skewers in water 30 minutes before using.

Prep time: 15 minutes plus marinating
Grilling time: 14 minutes

MARiNated SHish KABobs

Serve these grilled kabobs with pita bread wedges and couscous for a complete Mediterranean meal.

HERb-ROAsted LAMb

1 cup dry red wine

1 cup COLAVITA Extra Virgin
  Olive Oil

3 cloves garlic, minced

1 Tbsp. dried rosemary leaves

2 tsp. dried thyme leaves

1 tsp. *each salt and* pepper

1 butterflied leg of lamb
  (about 3 lb.)

MIX wine, oil, garlic and seasonings. Pour over lamb in large zipper-style plastic bag; seal bag. Marinate in refrigerator 2 hours or overnight, turning occasionally.

PLACE lamb on rack in roasting pan.

BAKE at 350°F for 40 to 50 minutes or until meat thermometer reaches 160°F (medium). Let stand 10 minutes before slicing. Serve with Quick & Easy Risotto (recipe, page 36) and garnish with fresh rosemary, if desired. Makes 8 servings.

Prep time: 5 minutes plus marinating
Baking time: 50 minutes plus standing

Marinades are a wonderful way to add flavor to lamb and other meats. This one, featuring extra virgin olive oil, red wine and herbs, makes butterflied leg of lamb a memorable meal when entertaining friends.

Hearty Athenian Stew

- **2 Tbsp. COLAVITA Extra Virgin Olive Oil**
- **2½ lb. beef *or* lamb stew meat**
- **1 large onion, sliced**
- **2 cans (28 oz. each) Italian-style plum tomatoes, undrained**
- **1 cup dry red wine**
- **½ cup chopped fresh parsley**
- **2 tsp. dried oregano leaves**
- **1 tsp. salt**

HEAT oil in large saucepan. Add meat and onion; cook until browned.

ADD remaining ingredients, breaking up tomatoes with back of spoon. Bring to a boil. Reduce heat to medium-low.

COOK, partially covered, 1 hour or until meat is tender. Serve over hot cooked rice, if desired. Makes 6 to 8 servings.

Prep time: 10 minutes
Cooking time: 1 hour

Savory Feta Burgers

Perk up a plain burger with ATHENOS Feta Cheese. The variety used here combines the Mediterranean flavors of basil and tomato along with the feta cheese.

- **1 lb. ground beef**
- **1 pkg. (8 oz.) ATHENOS Feta Cheese with Basil & Tomato, divided**
- **¼ tsp. fennel seed, crushed (optional)**
- **⅛ tsp. ground black pepper**

MIX meat, ½ of the cheese, crumbled, and seasonings. Shape into 4 patties.

GRILL, broil or fry 7 minutes on each side or until cooked through. Cut remaining cheese into 4 slices; place on top of burgers. Cook 1 to 2 minutes or until cheese begins to melt.

SERVE on Kaiser rolls with lettuce, tomato and onion slices, if desired. Makes 4 sandwiches.

Variation: Substitute ground lamb for half or all of the beef.

Prep time: 10 minutes
Grilling time: 16 minutes

The addition of wine, olives and artichokes to this classic Italian dish gives it a new twist that is sure to please.

SPANish Lasagna

MIX ricotta cheese, 2 cups of the mozzarella cheese, ½ cup of the Parmesan cheese and eggs; set aside. Mix spaghetti sauce, artichokes, olives and wine.

LAYER ⅓ of the sauce mixture, 3 lasagna noodles and ½ of the ricotta cheese mixture in 13x9-inch baking dish. Repeat layers. Top with remaining 3 noodles, remaining sauce mixture, 1 cup mozzarella cheese and ¼ cup Parmesan cheese.

BAKE at 350°F for 45 minutes. Let stand 10 minutes before serving. Makes 8 to 10 servings.

Note: Marinara sauce is a meatless spaghetti sauce, however, any spaghetti sauce can be used for this pasta dish.

Prep time: 20 minutes
Baking time: 45 minutes plus standing

1 **container (15 oz.) ricotta cheese**

3 **cups (12 oz.) shredded mozzarella cheese, divided**

¾ **cup (3 oz.) DI GIORNO Shredded Parmesan Cheese, divided**

2 **eggs, beaten**

1 **jar (28 oz.) spaghetti sauce with meat *or* marinara sauce**

1 **can (14 oz.) artichoke hearts, drained, chopped**

½ **cup sliced California ripe olives**

2 **Tbsp. dry red wine**

9 **lasagna noodles, cooked, drained**

Artichoke

Desserts

More often than not, Mediterranean meals end with a simple bowl of fruit. When those fruits are in great abundance, they're turned into compotes, baked into tarts or dried. Nuts are also an important part of the dessert repertoire. Here you'll find a variety of fruit and nut treats for adding a finishing touch to any meal, from a simple supper to a holiday celebration.

Savory Fruit Compote (recipe, page 80),

Toasted Walnut Biscotti (recipe, page 81)

SAVory FRuit COMPote

MIX wine, water, sugar and peel in medium saucepan. Add cinnamon stick. Bring to a boil.

STIR in fruit. Reduce heat to medium-low. Cook, uncovered, 30 minutes or until fruit is tender and the poaching liquid is slightly thickened.

SERVE warm or chilled with poaching liquid. Garnish with fresh herbs, if desired. Makes 8 servings.

Prep time: 5 minutes
Cooking time: 30 minutes

Photo, pages 78–79.

- 1 **cup dry white wine**
- 1 **cup water**
- ¾ **cup sugar**
- 1 **Tbsp. grated lemon peel**
- 1 **cinnamon stick**
- 2 **lb. mixed dried fruit (such as figs, dates, apricots, peaches, pears *and* prunes)**

The flavor-packed meals of the Mediterranean are best ended with a dessert that isn't overwhelming—and this compote fits the bill. Serve it simply as is or with a piece of Toasted Walnut Biscotti (recipe, opposite page).

It's an Italian tradition to eat these light and crispy cookies with a glass of dessert wine, but they also make a great mid-morning or dessert treat with coffee or tea.

Toasted Walnut Biscotti

- **2** cups flour
- **2** tsp. baking powder
- **¼** tsp. salt
- **½** cup (1 stick) butter *or* margarine, softened
- **⅔** cup sugar
- **1** tsp. vanilla
- **2** eggs
- **⅔** cup finely ground toasted California walnuts (see note, page 55)

MIX flour, baking powder and salt in small bowl. Beat butter, sugar and vanilla in large bowl with electric mixer on medium speed until light and fluffy. Add eggs, 1 at a time, beating well after each addition. Add flour mixture; mix well. Stir in toasted walnuts.

SHAPE dough into 3 (1½ inch wide) loaves on cookie sheet sprayed with no stick cooking spray. Bake at 350°F for 25 to 30 minutes or until golden brown. Remove from oven. Increase oven temperature to 375°F.

CUT loaves diagonally into ¾-inch slices. Place, cut-side down, on cookie sheet. Bake 8 to 10 minutes or until toasted and crisp. Makes 3 dozen.

Prep time: 20 minutes
Baking time: 40 minutes

Photo, pages 78–79.

Melo (may-LOW) means that the food contains honey. Serve this decadent dessert, inspired by the honey-flavored treats in Greek sweet shops, as the grand finale to a special meal.

Filling

- 4 pkg. (8 oz. each) **PHILADELPHIA BRAND Cream Cheese, softened**
- ⅔ cup honey
- ½ cup sugar
- 1 tsp. vanilla
- 4 eggs, beaten
- 2 tsp. *each* grated orange peel *and* lemon peel

Crust

- 2 cups California walnuts, toasted, cooled (see note, page 55)
- ¼ cup sugar
- ½ tsp. ground cinnamon

MIX cream cheese, honey, sugar and vanilla for filling with electric mixer on medium speed until well blended. Add eggs; mix until blended. Stir in peel.

PLACE walnuts, sugar and cinnamon for crust in food processor container fitted with steel blade; cover. Process until walnuts are finely ground.

PRESS crust mixture onto bottom of 9-inch springform pan. Pour filling mixture into prepared crust.

BAKE at 350°F for 50 to 55 minutes or until center is almost set. Loosen cake from rim of pan; cool before removing rim of pan. Refrigerate 3 hours or overnight. Garnish with orange slices, walnut pieces and orange leaves and drizzle with additional honey, if desired. Makes 12 servings.

Prep time: 15 minutes
Baking time: 55 minutes plus cooling and refrigerating

greek Melo cheesecake

Chocolate-Walnut Torta Caprese

Named for the famous Isle of Capri, this chocolate-nut cake is one of southern Italy's few chocolate desserts. After serving it, offer a cup of espresso for a finishing touch.

- ½ **cup (1 stick) butter *or* margarine, softened**
- ¾ **cup granulated sugar, divided**
- 8 **oz. semi-sweet chocolate, melted, cooled**
- 7 **eggs, separated**
- 1½ **cups ground California walnuts**
- ⅓ **cup flour**
  Powdered sugar

BEAT butter and ½ cup of the granulated sugar with electric mixer on medium speed until light and fluffy. Blend in cooled chocolate. Add egg yolks, 1 at a time, beating well after each addition. Toss walnuts and flour. Stir into butter mixture.

BEAT egg whites until foamy. Gradually add remaining ¼ cup granulated sugar, beating until soft peaks form. Stir ¼ of the egg whites into chocolate batter. Fold in remaining egg whites. Pour into 9-inch springform pan sprayed with no stick cooking spray.

BAKE at 350°F for 40 minutes or until toothpick inserted in center comes out clean. Cool in pan 10 minutes. Remove rim and cool completely. Sprinkle with powdered sugar. Garnish with additional walnut pieces and mint, if desired. Cut into wedges to serve. Makes 10 servings.

Prep time: 15 minutes
Baking time: 40 minutes plus cooling

Entertaining
SPANish TApas PARty

The custom of serving appetizers, called tapas (TAH-puhs), is popular all over Spain, but it is most typical in the Andalusia region of southern Spain. Casual, convivial snacks, tapas are not intended for intimate dining or fancy service. Most dishes are eaten with fingers or speared on toothpicks. A well-planned tapas menu offers a little bit of everything—something marinated, something saucy and something served on bread or in pastry.

To serve tapas, select simple serving dishes. Plain earthenware platters and casseroles are traditional. A hot tray or chafing dish will help keep the hot appetizers warm. Because tapas are finger foods, silverware isn't necessary, but toothpicks come in handy. Small plates are optional.

Sherry is the Spanish beverage traditionally served with tapas. The preferred sherry is a fino—pale, very dry sherry. Besides sherry, imported or domestic beer and dry red or white wine are excellent additions. Sangria, a fruity wine punch, makes a tasty beverage to serve with tapas as well.

Menu

Spicy Spanish Walnuts (page 14)
Marinated Olives (page 15)
Mediterranean Meatballs with Yogurt & Feta Sauce (page 25)
Hot & Spicy Artichoke Dip (page 23)
Choice of beverage
(such as sherry, beer, dry red or white wine, sangria
and/or non-alcoholic beverages)

Entertaining
Greek Easter Feast

Easter is an important religious holiday on the Greek calendar and a time for family gatherings. It is the meal that breaks the 40-day fast of Lent, during which no one is supposed to eat meat. Traditionally, the meal is eaten after midnight church services. On Easter, almost everyone in the nation eats the same entrée— roasted lamb.

For decorations, in the center of your Easter table should be a basket or bowl piled high with bright red eggs. It's customary for everyone to take an egg to break the Lenten fast.

On Holy Thursday, three days before Easter, some Greek homemakers bake tsoureki. Look for this sweetened egg bread at a Greek market, or you might be able to order it by mail. A selection of honeyed desserts is the usual finale to a Greek Easter meal. Along with the Greek Melo Cheesecake, you could pass plates of Greek honey-nut cookies.

Finally, be sure to serve feta cheese on your Easter meze platter. It can be an ingredient in a dip, or simply drizzled with olive oil and sprinkled with herbs.

Menu

Meze Platter (page 14)
ATHENOS® Greek Salad (page 51)
Tsoureki
Herb-Roasted Lamb (page 74)
Greek Melo Cheesecake (page 83)
Greek coffee or espresso

Entertaining
Italian Picnic

The Italians love to picnic. And no wonder they're so good at it—throughout the country, alfresco dining while conversing with family and friends is a popular pastime.

What to do on your picnic? Better take along your soccer ball, because soccer is the national sport. And people of all ages like to play bocce, a form of lawn bowling.

To pack your portable party, start out by dividing everything into three categories. Perishables, such as the appetizer and salad, should be kept in a cooler along with the wine. Food items that can stay at room temperature, including the biscotti and fruit, can go into a basket or cloth bag. Tableware should travel in something sturdy, with special care taken for the glasses.

For an extra-special touch, serve some of the items from rustic baskets lined with beautiful napkins and bring some votive candles to set out on pretty saucers. Buon appetito!

Menu

Torta Rustica (page 20)
White Bean & Tuna Salad (page 48)
Crusty loaf of Italian bread
Toasted Walnut Biscotti (page 81)
Fresh figs and peaches
Wine

Entertaining
Arabian Nights Dinner Party

Bring together foods and customs from the Middle East as well as North Africa for a magic carpet ride to another time and place.

Set the mood by lighting the room with candles in ornate brass candlesticks. Atop the white linens on your table, scatter pink and red rose petals. For serving, use brightly colored dishes with mosaic designs.

When you serve the couscous, explain to your guests that it is customary for everyone to eat it from a communal platter, using their fingers (better have the plates and forks ready, though).

After dinner, the brewing and serving of the mint tea is a traditional ritual of hospitality. The tea is usually prepared in a special brass or silver teapot and served in delicately etched tea glasses. You can create your own mint tea by brewing green tea with some fresh mint leaves and a little sugar.

Menu

ATHENOS® Hummus and 3-Pepper Hummus
Lahvosh (Armenian cracker bread)
Spicy Vegetable Couscous (page 33)
Marinated Shish Kabobs (page 72)
Savory Fruit Compote (page 80)
Mint tea

Eating the Mediterranean Way

The Pyramid: A Model for Healthy Eating

The Mediterranean Diet Pyramid can be a terrific tool to help plan a healthy and delicious diet. It's based on the historical and cultural eating habits of people living in certain parts of the Mediterranean region, specifically, southern Italy and France, as well as Greece, Spain and Turkey. Because these people have had, over time, lower incidence of coronary heart disease, their diet has naturally become a point of interest. Developed jointly by the Harvard School of Public Health, the United Nations World Health Organization and Oldways Preservation & Exchange Trust, the pyramid is a way to identify foods which make up a healthy diet, from a Mediterranean perspective. By adopting similar eating and lifestyle patterns, Americans may be able to improve their prospects for long-term health.

The Pyramid: A Delightful Design

One of the core principles of the Mediterranean Diet is to choose foods from the bottom section of the pyramid and then move up. Nutritionally speaking, this principle will design a diet higher in complex carbohydrates and lower in saturated fats. The pyramid visually shows the importance of the various food groups in the diet. In the bottom portion of the pyramid, we see grains, nuts, vegetables, fruits, olive oil, and cheese. Their position in the bottom means you should give emphasis to them and include these foods in your daily diet.

Better Eating: Block by Block

The grain group at the very bottom is high in complex carbohydrates, dietary fiber and B vitamins, and contains virtually no fat or saturated fat. Moving up the pyramid, the next most-important food group includes legumes, nuts, fruits and vegetables. Foods such as garbanzo beans and other dried beans, lentils, walnuts, olives, sesame seeds and minimally processed fruits and vegetables provide a wide assortment of nutrients. These include protein, dietary fiber, essential fatty acids, iron, zinc and vitamins A and C. Equally important is that some of the foods, such as nuts and olives, are a good source of monounsaturated fat. Studies with California walnuts have shown this kind of fat to have a beneficial effect on lowering blood cholesterol levels.

Going up on the pyramid, you'll see olive oil, cheeses and yogurt are also recommended on a daily basis. Like olives,

A few times per month

A few times per week

Daily

Wine in moderation

Exercise

Red meats

Sweets

Eggs

Poultry

Fish

Cheeses & yogurt

olive oil

Fruits, vegetables

Legumes & Nuts

Breads, Pasta, Rice, Couscous, Polenta, Bulgur & Other Grains

Source: ©1994 Oldways Preservation & Exchange Trust

olive oil primarily contains monounsaturated fat. Because of its cholesterol-lowering health benefits, and its delicious flavor, it is the oil of choice in Mediterranean cooking. Cheeses and yogurt can help meet daily requirements for calcium, which is an important mineral, especially for women.

And lastly, you'll see that animal-based foods, such as fish, poultry, eggs and red meats can be included on an occasional basis. So, too, can sweets. These groups do not necessarily have to be part of the daily diet.

The lifestyle Factor

Not to be overlooked are the recommendations appearing on the outside of the pyramid. Recent research indicates that moderate wine consumption provides some protective, heart-healthy benefits. Daily activity contributes to overall fitness and well-being. These two lifestyle recommendations, along with the pyramid foods, provide the ideal vehicle for mapping out your own Mediterranean-style approach to living.

Wine Guide

Buying Wine

When purchasing wine, you'll find most wines are available in 750 ml bottles; however, some are also bottled in magnums (1.5 l size). Plan on one 750 ml bottle for about five 5-ounce servings. A magnum will generally serve twice as many.

Types of Wines

Wines enjoyed before dinner, including dry sherry and vermouth, are known as apéritif wines. Dessert wines, such as cream sherry, Marsala and Ruby Port, are served with dessert or after a meal. Sparkling wines—champagne and spumante—can be served before, during or after a meal, and often are used to mark special occasions.

Table or dinner wines include white, red, and blush or rosé wines. White wines are light in body and flavor and can be dry and tart or sweet and fragrant. Red wines can be purple-red, brick-red or ruby-red. Red wines usually are dry and rich, sometimes with a tart or astringent quality. Blush or rosé wines are pink and can be either dry or sweet. Table wines also are appropriate to serve with appetizers.

Serving Wine

Just open the bottle of wine and pour. Most wines don't need to "breathe" and they don't need decanting (pouring into another container). However, consuming wine at the ideal serving temperature adds to the enjoyment of the wine. Serve red table wines at a cool room temperature (around 60° to 65°F); white wines cool, but not ice-cold (around 50°F); and blush or rosé wines, as well as sparkling wines, well chilled (somewhere between 40° to 50°F).

Don't worry about differentiating red wine glasses from white wine glasses. One good, all-purpose wine glass will do the trick, such as a 7- to 8-ounce tulip-shaped glass. However, for serving sparkling wines, the best glasses are flutes. Their tall, narrow shapes keep bubbles from escaping.

Storing Wine

For long-term storage, keep wine in a cool, well-ventilated place. The ideal temperature for storing wine is 55° to 60°F, but 10 degrees higher or lower is okay. Store a wine bottle that is sealed with a cork on its side to keep the cork moist.

Type	Flavor	Food Suggestions
WHITE TABLE WINES		
Chablis (shah-BLEE)	Dry; fresh & fruity	Oysters, light chicken dishes
Chardonnay (shahr-din-AY)	Dry; medium- to full-bodied	Seafood, pork, tuna, chicken
Chenin Blanc (SHEN-ihn BLAHNK)	Fresh & fruity; light-bodied	Brie, green grapes, seafood
Gewürztraminer (guh-VERT-strah-mee-nuhr)	Dry to semisweet; light-bodied; spicy	Spicy foods, gumbo
Pinot Blanc (PEE-noh BLAHNK)	Dry; slightly fruity; light-bodied	Seafood
White Riesling (REEZ-ling)	Dry to sweet; light-bodied	Light chicken dishes
Sauvignon Blanc (soh-veen-YOHN BLAHNK)	Dry & crisp; light- to medium-bodied	Goat cheese, seafood
Soave (SWAH-vay)	Dry; light-bodied	Seafood, fish, poultry, antipasto
RED TABLE WINES		
Bardolino (bahr-dihl-EE-noh)	Dry; light-bodied	Turkey, fish, veal, risotto, pizza
Beaujolais Nouveau (boh-zhoh-LAY noo-VOH)	Young & fruity; light-bodied	Chicken, steak
Burgundy	Medium- to heavy-bodied	Beef stew, duck
Bordeaux (bohr-DOH)	Light & fresh to strong & hard-edged	Lamb, hard cheeses
Cabernet Sauvignon (kah-buhr-NAY soh-veen-YOHN)	Rich & dry; medium- to full-bodied	Game dishes, roast beef
Chianti (kee-AHN-tee)	Dry & fruity; medium-bodied	Lamb
Lambrusco (lahm-BROO-skoh)	Dry to slightly sweet & fruity	Robust tomato-sauced pastas
Merlot (mehr-LOH)	Dry; light- to full-bodied	Lamb, veal, strong cheeses, steak, lasagna
Pinot Noir (PEE-noh NWAHR)	Spicy & smooth; rich; light-bodied	Salmon, strong cheeses
Zinfandel (ZIHN-fuhn-dehl)	Light- to strong-bodied	Paté, steak, veal
BLUSH OR ROSÉ WINES		
Grenache (gruh-NAHSH)	Dry to semisweet	Light main courses
White Zinfandel (ZIHN-fuhn-dehl)	Slightly sweet	Pizza, nachos, fried chicken
SPARKLING WINES		
Champagne (shahm-PAYN)	Very dry to sweet	Appetizers
Spumante (spoo-MAHN-tay)	Sweet & fruity	Sweet desserts

INdex

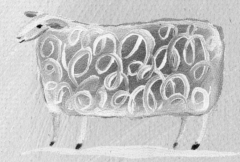

CREDITS

Project Leader: Sara Owens, Churny Company, Inc.

Brand Representatives: ATHENOS and DI GIORNO—Sheri Petras
      California Olive Industry—Dave Daniels
      California Walnuts—Stephen H. Zimmerman, East
        West Promotions
      COLAVITA Olive Oil—Anthony Profaci

Recipe Development: Lisa Brandt-Whittington, Kraft Creative Kitchens

Produced By: Meredith Custom Publishing

Metric Conversions

Metric Cooking Hints

By making a few conversions, cooks in Australia, Canada, and the United Kingdom can use the recipes in *Culinary Journey to the Mediterranean* with confidence. The charts on this page provide a guide for converting measurements from the U.S. customary system, which is used throughout this book, to the imperial and metric systems. There also is a conversion table for oven temperatures to accommodate the differences in oven calibrations.

Product Differences: Most of the ingredients called for in the recipes in this book are available in English-speaking countries. However, some are known by different names. Here are some common American ingredients and their possible counterparts:
• Sugar is granulated or castor sugar.
• Powdered sugar is icing sugar.
• All-purpose flour is plain household flour or white flour. When self-rising flour is used in place of all-purpose flour in a recipe that calls for leavening, omit the leavening agent (baking soda or baking powder) and salt.
• Light-colored corn syrup is golden syrup.
• Cornstarch is cornflour.
• Baking soda is bicarbonate of soda.
• Vanilla is vanilla essence.
• Green, red or yellow sweet peppers are capsicums.
• Golden raisins are sultanas.

Volume and Weight: Americans traditionally use cup measures for liquid and solid ingredients. The chart, above right, shows the approximate imperial and metric equivalents. If you are accustomed to weighing solid ingredients, the following approximate equivalents will be helpful.
• 1 cup butter, castor sugar, or rice = 8 ounces = about 250 grams
• 1 cup flour = 4 ounces = about 125 grams
• 1 cup icing sugar = 5 ounces = about 150 grams
   Spoon measures are used for smaller amounts of ingredients. Although the size of the tablespoon varies slightly in different countries, for practical purposes and for recipes in this book, a straight substitution is all that's necessary.
   Measurements made using cups or spoons always should be level unless stated otherwise.

Equivalents: U.S. = Australia/U.K.

⅛ teaspoon = 0.5 ml	⅔ cup = ½ cup = 5 fluid ounces = 150 ml
¼ teaspoon = 1 ml	¾ cup = ⅔ cup = 6 fluid ounces = 180 ml
½ teaspoon = 2 ml	1 cup = ¾ cup = 8 fluid ounces = 240 ml
1 teaspoon = 5 ml	1¼ cups = 1 cup
1 tablespoon = 1 tablespoon	2 cups = 1 pint
¼ cup = 2 tablespoons = 2 fluid ounces = 60 ml	1 quart = 1 litre
⅓ cup = ¼ cup = 3 fluid ounces = 90 ml	½ inch =1.27 cm
½ cup = ⅓ cup = 4 fluid ounces = 120 ml	1 inch = 2.54 cm

Baking Pan Sizes

American	Metric
8x1½-inch round baking pan	20x4-centimetre cake tin
9x1½-inch round baking pan	23x3.5-centimetre cake tin
11x7x1½-inch baking pan	28x18x4-centimetre baking tin
13x9x2-inch baking pan	30x20x3-centimetre baking tin
2-quart rectangular baking dish	30x20x3-centimetre baking tin
15x10x1-inch baking pan	30x25x2-centimetre baking tin (Swiss roll tin)
9-inch pie plate	22x4- or 23x4-centimetre pie plate
7- or 8-inch springform pan	18- or 20-centimetre springform or loose-bottom cake tin
9x5x3-inch loaf pan	23x13x7-centimetre or 2-pound narrow loaf tin or paté tin
1½-quart casserole	1.5-litre casserole
2-quart casserole	2-litre casserole

Oven Temperature Equivalents

Fahrenheit Setting	Celsius Setting*	Gas Setting
300°F	150°C	Gas Mark 2 (slow)
325°F	160°C	Gas Mark 3 (moderately slow)
350°F	180°C	Gas Mark 4 (moderate)
375°F	190°C	Gas Mark 5 (moderately hot)
400°F	200°C	Gas Mark 6 (hot)
425°F	220°C	Gas Mark 7
450°F	230°C	Gas Mark 8 (very hot)
Broil		Grill

* Electric and gas ovens may be calibrated using Celsius. However, for an electric oven, increase the Celsius setting 10 to 20 degrees when cooking above 160°C. For convection or forced-air ovens (gas or electric), lower the temperature setting 10°C when cooking at all heat levels.